MOTHER WOVE THE MORNING

a one-woman play by

Carol Lynn Pearson

PEARSON PUBLISHING

All inquiries regarding this play should be addressed to:
Mother Wove the Morning
1384 Cornwall Ct.
Walnut Creek, CA 94596.

A video of Carol Lynn Pearson performing this play is available and can be ordered from the address above, as can other copies of the book, or by calling (510) 906-8835.

Cover photo by Ted Macke; Illustration by Shauna Cook Clinger; Design by Yvonne M. Wright.

Printed on recycled paper.

Library of Congress Cataloging-in-Publication Data

Pearson, Carol Lynn.
    Mother wove the morning : a one-woman play / by
Carol Lynn Pearson.
        p. cm.
    ISBN 1-56236-307-7
    1. Women—History—Drama. I. Title.
PS3566.E227M68   1992
812'.54—dc20   92-31236
                                                CIP

To my mother Emeline
To your mother
and most especially
To the Mother of us all

Introduction

Mother Wove the Morning is the product of a lifetime of hunger and searching and discovery. I grew up in Provo, Utah, grand-daughter of numerous Mormon pioneers. Life was good and secure and the mountains were clean and the neighbors were kind and opportunities were abundant. God was in his heaven and all was right with the world.

"His heaven."

I remember saying at nine years of age, as I walked with a friend on a country road one evening, "Well, there's one good thing about being a woman — at least you don't have to marry one!"

Where did I get that idea? I was getting top grades in school and was always "teacher's pet." My mother was a successful and respected school teacher. I felt myself to be the favorite child of my father, who had three sons and two daughters. Nobody ever told me I couldn't do something because I was a girl. I was constantly told that God loved me. But for nine years I had lived in a world in which the subliminal negative messages about being female were everywhere.

Without being told, I was being *clearly* told that maleness was a superior commodity. In society there was no question. It was a man's world. And at church. God's world was a man's world too. The heavenly beings we sang praise to were all male. Every prayer we uttered was to a male and through a male. God's prophets, ancient and modern, were male. His crowning creation, Adam, was male.

Even the stories in Sunday School were almost always about boys or men. People in the Bible prayed for sons, never for daughters. Every act of religious importance needed the authority that only males had. It was as clear as the vertical line on the blackboard: "God — man — woman." Eve and I were a beloved support, but we were auxiliary. God's house was designed and furnished and owned by males and it was a Motherless house. There were no feminine touches anywhere.

However, there was one tiny window in the dark patriarchal space that my eye could not resist. Joseph Smith, the founder of my church, had taught that we have not only a Heavenly Father, but a Heavenly Mother as well. I stared at that tiny window, transfixed. What wonders might be beyond it?

On July 31, 1961, as a twenty-one year-old, I wrote the following in my diary.

This evening I began . . . reading *Women of Mormondom* by Edward W. Tullidge. I skimmed over a few comments, and then lighted upon this paragraph on p. 177:

"Presently woman herself shall sing of her divine origin. A high-priestess of the faith shall interpret the themes of herself and of her Father-and-Mother God!"

The most glorious dream that I have ever dared to let play upon my consciousness is that of, in some way, discovering and singing the divine existence of woman . . . My soul cries out almost audibly — with an overpowering desire both to experience and to reclaim the rightful fulfillment of woman's creation . . . Whether or not I bear the potential of being a "high priestess" able to sing the themes of womanhood and my "Father-and-Mother-God" to ears other than my own — at least I shall sing them to myself.

I have since learned that many "high-priestesses" and "high priests" of many faiths — have stared, as I had, at the little window in their own tradition that invited them to consider the forgotten feminine divine. I love to hear their stories. But back to my own.

Holding my breath, I climbed out the window. And the view was stunning. So many witnesses — history, archeology, anthropology, philology, mythology (not to mention common sense) — told me the same story. The human family has *not* always viewed God as male. The earliest accounts speak of God as Mother. What happened? I could not read fast enough. Delight and rage filled me together — delight to learn that male supremacy was a male invention — and rage that no one had ever told me this before, rage that I had been allowed to grow up female in a Motherless house.

By 1982 my research filled a large cardboard box, but it was put away. Other projects seemed more pressing and were certainly safer, and by this time the demands of four children were enormous. But one afternoon, as I was taking a nap, I had a dream. I have never had a "vision" or heard a "voice," but I do have dreams that come I believe from my own spiritual resources. In this dream I had been told that my mother, who in actual reality died when I was fifteen, was really alive and being kept at the home of my step-mother. I rushed to the house and my three brothers told me that our mother was in a certain closet. I entered and saw at the top of a shelf a large cardboard box. I climbed up and peeked into it. There was the head of my mother, with her eyes closed. I studied her, wondering if she were dead or alive. Suddenly her eyes opened and she said, "Well, it's about time you got here!"

My message to myself could not have been more clear. It was about time I took "off the shelf" and "out of the closet" the Mother project. The Mother was not dead, but very much alive and only waiting for the children to find her. Immediately I got out my box of research and began.

But it was years before I found the right vehicle. One day in early 1989, as I was walking in the hills near my home, the Mother project fell into place in a totally unexpected way: it would be a play, a one-woman play. In it I would embody the women I had met in my search, women who could help to solve the mystery of the loss of the Mother and invite her home. I hadn't been on the stage for twenty-five years, but I thought, "I've got to do it!"

I selected the women, wrote, rewrote, rented our community theatre, chose props, costume, blocked, memorized, advertised — and did it.

My very first performance came two days after the major Northern California earthquake in October of 1989. As I hung onto the door frame while the house was rolling, I prayed, "Dear Father and Mother, please don't let me die before I can do my play even *one time!*"

I have now performed my play well over two hundred times, and my constant prayer is, "Dear Mother and Father, I am *so grateful* I get to do this thrilling thing. Thank you, thank you, thank you!"

There are no words to express the level of my gratitude for the privilege of participating in one of the most important shifts that is occurring on the planet today. The reclaiming of the feminine has profound implications for all aspects of society, touching intimately the way we relate to ourselves, to each other, to the earth and to God.

I extend my thanks to each person who has come to a performance of *Mother Wove the Morning*, for helping to create those sacred moments in which the theatre has served as a place of spiritual ritual, where together we have moved toward healing, toward wholeness and holiness. To the young woman who told me she was a victim of incest and that her life from that moment on would be transformed. To the elderly gentleman who embraced me in tears and said, "There are no words to tell you what this evening meant to me." To the young man who handed me a poem after his fourth time at the play: "If you listen you can hear sixteen women singing through her, and sixty billion humming along." To the elderly woman who said, "I didn't think I'd live long enough to see what I've seen tonight." To the Catholic priest who said, "I realize for the first time the harm we have done to women and to the Mother." To the young Jewish girl who said, "Your play made me feel so warm inside, so proud to be a woman." To the thousands of women and men — Catholic, Mormon, Presbyterian, Mennonite, Christian of all types, Jewish, Sikh, Muslim, and atheist — who have greeted me with such enthusiastic appreciation.

The Mother is returning, in our hearts and in our minds, and eventually in our worship. After every performance someone has said to me, "Let me tell you what my church is doing to bring back the Mother." Or "This is what my group is doing." *Every* religion is dealing with the issue, some enthusiastically, some reluctantly, some determined not to acknowledge the need. The potency of this issue, and the profound change in our thinking that it requires, is such that a backlash of fear and punishment is very much present. But more powerful is the wave of progress and change that is so evident and so desperately needed.

I anticipate in my hopes and my dreams a time in years to come — who knows how many? — possibly fewer than we thought — in which women and men move solidly toward partnership together, acknowledging in our own way the partnership of our Father and Mother God. In that day we will speak of and sing of and speak to a Creator in whose image we *all* are made equally. We will look at one another with a new reverence, and "women's work" will be given a respect that is more than lip service. So many of the ills of our society — such as today's increasing violence toward women and the horrors of incest — will be alleviated, for half of humanity will no longer be elevated over the other half because they are thought to be closer to God and his image and his authority.

To you who hold this book in your hand, I offer my hand, grateful to be with you on this splendid journey.

Carol Lynn Wright Pearson
August, 1992
Walnut Creek, California

"The Mother Goddess is virtually universal as the
dominant figure in the most ancient stories . . .
the female force was recognized as
awesome, powerful, transcendent . . .
We have seen how men appropriated and then
transformed . . . the power of the Mother Goddess."
Gerda Lerner, *The Creation of Patriarchy*

"The God of Judaism is undoubtedly a father-
symbol . . . nor can there be any doubt
as to the need answered by this image . . .
however, there is an equally great,
or possibly even greater need for yet another
symbol: that of the divine woman who appears in
many different forms throughout the world yet
remains basically the same everywhere."
Raphael Patai, *The Hebrew Goddess*

"The more than usually miserable state of the world
demands that the supreme Godhead be redefined,
that the repressed desire of the Western races for
some practical form of goddess worship be satisfied."
Robert Graves, *The White Goddess*

ast of Characters

ACT ONE

Carol Lynn Pearson ....Today

Bruen the Paleolithic..............................20,000 B.C.

Rachel and the Teraphim...........................1600 B.C.

Helah the Midianite Virgin........................1300 B.C.

Amenepshut the Egyptian Priestess...........1200 B.C.

Lydia and the Rape of the Levite's Concubine..1000 B.C.

Io the Greek ....475 B.C.

Julia the Gnostic ....200 A.D.

Paula the Christian at Ephesus....................431 A.D.

ACT TWO

Genevieve the Witch 1432

Running Cloud the Native American................1600

Phoebe the Shaker 1825

Emma Smith the Mormon First Lady...............1842

Elizabeth Cady Stanton the American Feminist ..1870

Hilda the Nazi Woman 1942

Rebecca the Jewish Woman............................1942

Marie the Therapist ....Today

Carol Lynn Pearson ....Today

ct One

Carol Lynn Pearson

Well, it seems the Pope dies and goes to heaven, and St. Peter greets him saying, "Before you come in we have this little test you have to pass. You have to spell the word 'God.'" Of course, he does and he goes in. Then Billy Graham dies and goes to heaven, and St. Peter greets him saying, "Before you come in, we have this little test you have to pass. You have to spell the word 'God.'" He does, and he goes in. Then Barbara Harris — that's the first female Episcopal bishop — dies and goes to heaven, and St. Peter greets her saying, "Before you come in we have this little test you have to pass." And she says, "Oh, no! Not another test! That's all I've done down there — pass this test and that test. And you know the tests are always harder for the women than they are for the men!" And St. Peter says, "Don't be silly, my dear. Spell 'Melchizedek.'"

I thank you for laughing at my joke. You see, there are sixteen women backstage here, some of whom are suffering severe stage fright right now — others of whom cannot *wait* for their turn to get out here. Like me. Do you know how excited I am to be able to do my play for you tonight, and how grateful I am to all of you for coming? I thank you.

Now, speaking of God — and of being a woman — which we are going to be doing in this play, I once met the man who played the voice of God in "The Ten Commandments." I did. His name was Delos Jewkes, and he had a voice — well, you remember his voice — like the Grand Canyon. Of course they chose him. It would be hard to imagine Cecil B. De Mille holding auditions for God and saying, "Now, that Jewkes fellow. Voice is a little too . . . . Listen, would you call Katharine Hepburn and see if she's available?" Wouldn't that have been great!

A little girl once wrote a letter, "Dear God, are boys really better than girls? I know you are one, but try to be fair."

When I was young, I wrote a poem about living in a Motherless house, where kindest patriarchal care does not ease the pain, where I bury my face in something soft as a breast, where I am a child, crying for my Mother in the night.

But you see, in my heart I know that the Creator that brought us here is in some wonderful way both Father and Mother — that perhaps, in the beginning, on that primordial day, Mother wove the morning and Father made the evening, joyfully, together. Why, then, did I grow up feeling that my world was a Motherless house?

On December tenth, 1963, and I know because I checked my diary, I ran through the rain by myself to the Jerusalem museum. And I stood there open-mouthed as the museum director pointed out certain artifacts as showing the transition from worship of the female to worship of the male. I was dumb-founded. The Goddess — under glass.

One more story. On Mother's Day of 1982 —

yes, I do keep a very good diary — after I finished
the breakfast in bed that my children brought me, I
told the four of them I wanted them to sit with me
for a little and talk about God.

Aaron groaned. Emily punched him. "Aaron,
it's *Mother's Day!*"

"Okay, Emily," I said, "you first. I want you
to close your eyes and tell me what you see when
you think of God."

"Okay. Well, then—I see a man—he's pretty
old—he's dressed in a long robe, and he has a very
stern expression on his face."

"Do you like him?"

"I — I don't think he likes me. I know he's
supposed to love me, but he's telling me that if I'm
not good when the millennium comes, I'll get burnt
to a crisp."

I felt my heart break. Fourteen years old.

And even if she had found her picture of God
warm and inviting, which I know God surely to be,
there he was — totally male. And there she was —
the other — as I had been, the other. And as so
many millions of women had been.

I began to think about all those women. Did
they know anything I didn't know? Oh, I wanted
to find them, to see through their eyes. So I went
out searching. I walked backward in time. I
walked through their villages and courtyards and
homes and dungeons, crying out, "Where is my
Mother? Nobody can tell me you can have a
Father without a Mother. Did she abandon us on
the doorstep without even a note?"

And as quiet as ghosts, some of my sisters
appeared, and they began to speak to me. And the

things they told me have turned my life upside down. Or, I think, right side up. And I knew that you would be just as interested as I was, and so they and I sat down and put together this play for you, and all of it, to the best of their knowledge and mine, is true.

A few months ago I picked up this newspaper from my porch and I read a little headline I will never forget as long as I live. "Sixty Million Missing Women Tell Bias Toll." Did any of you see this? The historical preference for males over females has left an amazing disparity in the statistics of a recently completed census in developing countries. Sixty million women are missing — because of female infanticide, selective abortion, little girls being given not the same food or medical treatment as their brothers. And the estimate is worldwide — more than one hundred million gone because they were born or about to be born female. Well, we are still rightly horrified that just decades ago six million were killed because they were Jewish. What can our minds even do with these numbers?

I will put this article with my others — I have so many — on rape, battered women, bride burning in India because of insufficient dowry increasing, not decreasing, eighty million women in Africa subjected to sexual mutilation. It goes on and on, and one finally has to say, "What is wrong with this picture?" One clue — in the words of a Catholic theologian: "If God is male, the male is god."

Well, shall we dedicate this evening's performance to these one hundred million women who ought to be breathing today?

You will have to stretch your mind back
many thousands of years.
You can. Anything is possible here.
This is the theatre. Seats for you. Stage for me.
Light — to help us all see a little more clearly.
This evening see, in your own way — the Goddess
— God the Mother—the female face of God.
Or, if you like, call her the Feminine Archetype.

We begin in the paleolithic.
Bruen, an ancient ancestress of ours,
walks the clean earth
and hears the echo of my question.

Bruen
the Paleolithic

I do not understand. You lost Mother?
Is not possible!
Listen, her voice — wind. You have wind?
Feel. Earth — her womb, giving, giving. Seasons,
her cycle. Look, moon — her silver egg, fruit of
her night sky. Stars, her eyes. Rain, her good
milk. You have heavens? You have Mother.
You have woman, who by magic bleeds, by
magic swells, opens to bear child? You have Mother.
You have little figurines with great belly,
breasts?
Her holy blood on your floors stained with
ocher?
Her image on walls of your caves? Of course!
You tell your children story, yes? In
beginning she was there, Goddess of All Things,
and she rose naked from chaos. But nothing was
for her feet to rest upon, so she divided sea from
sky. She danced lonely upon waves. Wind as she
danced began work of creation. From herself she
formed heavens, earth, all in them. You tell story
to your children, yes?
You have high priestess, who speaks to
Goddess for you and to you for Goddess? And

who makes earth fertile each year by choosing
fortunate lover from among men and enjoying with
him sacred marriage, then giving him as offering to
Goddess that she may enjoy him too.

   You have all this, yes?

   Ah—you do not?

   You *have* lost Mother!   I worry now for you.
Mother — is all!

   Mmmm — you said word — "fa-ther."   What
is this?

Do you remember Rachel in the Bible?
That's Mrs. Jacob of Abraham, Isaac, and?
We find her early one morning in her tent
near to the hill country of Gilead.

Rachel and the Teraphim

Who told you I have them? Is this what you seek, the teraphim, the little images of the gods and goddesses I have taken? You seek them too, like my father Laban seeks them? Listen. He shouts now in the tent of the maidservants. "Where are the teraphim?" he shouts. "Where are my gods and goddesses?" Oh, listen to him shout! And if he finds them with me, I will pay with my life!

But he will not find them. See? I place myself on the camel cushion, my skirts like so, and under my skirts I hide the teraphim, the little images I have taken. Oh, you are saying, that is too easy, her father will find them.

Oh, no! No. You wait and see.

You think I am a robber? I steal because they are mine and my right to hold them has been stolen from me, as right after right has been stolen from me. But these — these I steal back again — to help me remember.

In the days of Sarah, grandmother to my husband Jacob and wife to Abraham, the ways of the mothers still prevailed. Sarah was a priestess, a prophetess of power, the mother, the Matriarch, and she knew the old ways, the ancient order in which the mothers were honored and all the people blessed. But the new ways came, the customs that honored the fathers and exacted obedience to them. We have stories of wandering nomads that came on horses with their thrusting weapons of bronze in their hands to kill and take slaves. Theirs was a god of war and mountain, a male without a female, and with them the peace of the mothers vanished from the earth — woman became property — cities had walls.

Oh, I remember Sarah, and I bless her name! But the names of the mothers are being erased—as if written by a finger on the desert floor before a wind — and my seed, I fear, will not know the name of my mother, or the name of the Goddess of Mesopotamia, for whom I was named Rachel, "Mother of the Holy Lamb." I leave the land of the Goddess to go to the land of the patriarchs. But I carry with me, hidden here beneath my skirts, her memory and her hope.

Do you hear him? Now he is in the tent of my sister Leah. "Where are my teraphim?" Shhhhh!

My father, you know, has traveled a seven days' journey to find us, for we left without his knowledge when he had gone to shear his sheep. And this morning I listened from my tent as he said to my husband Jacob, "Why have you stolen my gods?"

And Jacob said, and he spoke truly, "I have not stolen your gods. Come in and search. And if you find them with any one of us, that person shall not live!"

It is true. My husband Jacob, who cried and kissed me on the first day we met, who loves me and worked fourteen years to obtain me — he will see that I am killed if the teraphim are found. So. You may think it strange. For the sacred images I would risk my life? There is more to life, you know, than breath. A life that has given up its meaning is not a life. A life that has given up its power is not a life. These little goddesses and gods I hide beneath my skirt — mine by the matrilineal prerogative — are my meaning and my power, and without them what good would my life be to me?

But my life will be spared, and I will tell you why. In a moment my father will come to my tent to search and I will say to him, "Father, forgive me that I cannot rise before you, for the period of women is upon me." And my father will not come near to me, for if he were to touch me he would be unclean and accursed!

(Laughs) The ancient ways of the mothers — the curse of the woman — will save my life!

You see, about once, every century or two,

it comes in handy, women!

Well, really, much more often

if we would stop to consider this great gift.

elah the Midianite Virgin

I'm just going to have to tell you about this next woman because I can't get her out here. Well, she's only ten years old. You read about her in the Bible. She's one of the Midianite virgins taken as booty by the warrior priests of Israel. She wrote this note, said I could read it to you if I wanted.

"Tell them — I still remember the blood of my mother on my robe.

"The men of Israel killed my father and all the men of the city and the five kings and all the little brothers. They looked at the bodies of the women and the girls, and those that had known man were put to the sword, and those that had not known man were given to the men of Israel on the plains of Moab by Jordan.

"I do not know why they hated us so. They said our god was false and our god was evil and our god was a woman, and theirs was the only true god and he hated the female god and said that men must rule over women.

"My mother held me close until they tore her from my arms and ran the sword through her belly. Whenever I close my eyes I see her blood on my robe. Tell them I am sorry I could not come, but I would cry and be ashamed."

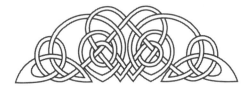

An oasis appears. Egypt.

Amenepshut the Egyptian Priestess

There he goes again! Did you hear him? The high priest shook his finger in my face and argued that we must have more priests than priestesses serving here in the temple at Memphis because men are nearer the form of the divine than are women!

"What?" I said. "Nearer the form of Isis, oldest of the old, the Goddess from whom all being arose?"

"Ah!" he said, smiling with some vast, superior wisdom, "that was a misconception. The great god Ptah was before Isis and is more powerful."

They are always doing that to us, bringing in one god or another and claiming he was here first! Now, why? Why this wanting a male in the heavens? What difference can it make?

Well. "Absurd!" I said to the high priest, shaking my finger in *his* face. "Who gave birth to Ptah?"

"No one," he said. "Ptah gave birth to all the gods and the goddesses."

"Oh? And how did he, a *male*, accomplish this marvel?"

Well, I blush to tell you. Ptah — the high priest told me! — performed a certain act upon himself, and there issued all — all of creation!

Excuse me, I must make this right with Isis. And I'm glad she has a sense of humor!

I've got to take a few deep breaths
before I get this next woman out here.
Sometimes I wake up in the night with her voice
going around and around in my head.

Lydia and the Rape of the Levite's Concubine

Shhhh! I do not want them to hear. When they hear me talking to myself as I sit here in the kitchen by the fire, my brother's wife shouts at me, "Old Woman, be quiet!" And she tells me again that I am mad, that I have been mad since I was thirteen. And then my brother comes and puts an arm around me and weeps to see me so. For he remembers the day as I do.

I will tell you the story. She will not let me tell it, but if I am quiet — if you are quiet — she will never know, will she?

It is when I am thirteen and I am my mother's jewel. We live in Gibeah, which belongs to the tribe of Benjamin.

My mother and I have secrets. We go sometimes to the high place under the spreading trees where the Asherah is planted, the carved wooden pole of the Goddess, the remembrance of her that Created All Things, and my mother tells me the stories of the ancient ones who knew her. My father knows not of this, for he listens to the priests of those who hate the Goddess and call her an abomination. And so my mother and I have secrets.

One day my father brought home with him a man who wore the scarlet and violet robes and the grand headdress and the gold and precious gems and perfume of the Levite priest, one of the chosen, ruling priesthood of the great god Jaweh. And my father said, "Look, here is a Levite priest who has no lodging but the street, and he will be my guest, him and his asses and his concubine."

And so my father and the man made merry. And the concubine told my mother and me her heart as we prepared the food and the drink.

Her name was Adah and she was of Bethlehem of Judah. She had long black hair and soft, sad eyes, and skin like the skim part of the milk, and she was but one year older than I. Her father, she told us, had sold her as concubine to the Levite priest, but she hated him and ran away back to her father's house. But the Levite came again to bring her, and she wept, but her father was glad, for she was no longer a virgin and of no value to him. So she was put on the ass the Levite had brought, and here she was, and where could she run to now?

When it was dark there came a loud beating at the door, and I heard some men cry out, "Bring to us now the man that came into your house, that we may know him."

And I heard my father say, "No! No, Brethren, do not so wickedly."

"Bring him!" they shouted.

Then the door to my room flew open and my father laid hold upon me with one hand and upon Adah with the other, and he brought us to the door of the house and he said, "Look! Here is my daughter, a maiden, and the concubine of the man you seek. Do to them as you wish, but to this man, this man of God, do not so vile a thing."

Then my mother fell upon us both and she said, "Old man, leave the girl alone! This is my jewel, my only daughter!"

My mother ran with me out the back of the house, and her hand on my arm shook like a leaf of the Asherah, but it was strong, strong, and we ran. We ran to the high place near our house and we hid in the little grove of sacred trees and we knelt before the Goddess and pled for her mercy!

Soon we heard the scream of Adah and we looked to see as she was carried by the men from our house to the foot of the high place where we were, and they did not see us and they did not hear us, for our hands were over our mouths.

Ah, can I tell it?

They humbled her! Oh, they lay her on the ground and one by one they performed their wickedness upon her. They laughed and tried to outdo each other with their vileness. My mother held me close so I could hardly breathe and whispered that I should keep my eyes on the Asherah and not look at their sins. Ah, but the moans that filled our ears! Ah, the pitiful cries of Adah for her mother, for her father, for whatever God had ears to hear! All, all through the night!

When the dawning came and the men had finished with her, they stood back and said, "Go, then." And they watched and we watched as Adah crawled to the door of our house. And when she reached the threshold, she could go no further, and she lay unmoving, and her black hair covered the step.

The men left to go to their houses, and we were about to go to Adah, when — her lord the

Levite came from our house and saw that his concubine had fallen down at the step.

"Up," he said, "let us be going."

But she did not answer.

Then he spoke again, but still she did not answer. Then he bent down to see, then rose and said, "Well, she is dead. Bring the ass."

There, I have said it! But can I tell the rest? Adah's lord the Levite, when he had arrived at his house by the side of Mount Ephraim, took his concubine Adah and divided her with a knife into twelve pieces and sent one piece to each of the tribes with a message calling for vengeance — though he himself had slept soundly that whole night long!

For years whenever my father told a visitor of how he saved the life of the man of God, I would begin to growl low under my breath and he would make me leave the room.

I leave the kitchen now only to go to my bed. I do not even go to the high place. In my youth I thought she was in the green of the trees we planted to her name, this Goddess you seek, giving us some memory of a day when woman was favored and promising that we will again be remembered. When I was thirteen I decided she was in the heavens hiding from her Lord the Levite and speaking low and trying not to offend.

But now I am old, and I know that if ever there was a Goddess in the heavens, she was long ago cast down, down to be trodden and abused, and to be told, "Old Woman, be quiet!"

So she sits with me by the fire here, see? — and we rock together and we gossip and whisper. And no one notices us much, for we are women — and we are old women — and maybe we are — mad women!

She does that to me every time.
I've asked her if she can't leave out some of those
places, and she tells me no, she can't,
so I just let her . . . .

o
the Greek

I attended the theatre this afternoon. The entire city of Athens is invited — required — men, women, slaves, to attend the theatre. I would have enjoyed being down there on the stage holding a mask! (Raises fan as mask and intones in a deep voice) I think I have a good voice. (Mask down) But of course, only men may act.

And so — I am a listener.

The play was "The Eumenides" by Aeschylus. Orestes is on trial for having killed his mother, Clytemnestra, after she avenges the death of her daughter, Iphigenia. And the god Apollo takes it upon himself to argue, in Orestes behalf, that he could not possibly have killed his mother, for children are not related to their mothers! For — (Mask up) "The mother is no parent of that which is called her child. She is only nurse to the new planted seed that grows, whose true parent is the male." (Mask down)

I looked around me. All, men, women, stared unblinking at this remarkable assertion. They had just been told that the sun above them, moving in its ordained course toward the mountains, was really the moon. And they sat there unblinking!

But I cannot fault them, for they have been carefully taught, and not everyone sees beyond the stage, as I do, or hears more than is said.

And Apollo continued. (Mask up) "I will prove to you now that there can be a father without any mother. There she stands, the living witness, daughter of Olympian Zeus." (Mask down)

Enter — Athena, whom our religion tells us sprang forth full blown from the forehead of her father Zeus. And Athena says, (Mask up) "Apollo is right. Only fathers are related to their children." (Mask down) Can you tell this is a man speaking behind the mask of a woman? I thought so. I mean, really! (Mask up) "I am always for the male with all my heart, and strongly on my father's side." (Mask down)

And then the chorus, the Furies — oh, that's who I would have played, that's who I *am* — exclaim in horror, (Mask up) "Gods of the younger generation, you have ridden down the laws of the elder time, torn them out of my hands!" (Mask down)

The laws of the elder time. Athena was not always Zeus' daughter, did you know that? She and the other goddesses were sovereign in the heavens as woman was sovereign on earth. And then came the thunderbolt god Zeus, who overturned the order of the heaven as man overturned the order of the earth, and which happened first I do not know — do you?

There never has been and there never will be a man who was not born of woman! And are they so envious that they take to themselves even this most obvious reality of nature? Woman, they would have us believe, was really born of man, as Athena was born of the forehead of Zeus. Or, as a traveler told me, it is somewhere taught — that woman was born of a man's rib!

And the sun is really the moon!

Well, do you wonder whether Orestes was pronounced guilty? The jury of twelve Athenian citizens was evenly divided, and so Athena, the goddess herself, cast the deciding vote.

May I see by the uplifted hand those who think the goddess voted for the reality of motherhood? Hands? And those who think she voted against herself? Hands? You are right! Athena sided with the men, didn't she? Orestes is acquitted on the ground that he could not have shed kindred blood, for indeed he had no mother!

And we left the theatre to go to our homes, fully aware of who has been born of whom, of what happens to a woman who dares to rebel as Clytemnestra rebelled, and of the place in this world of goddess and woman.

Well, if Athena declares for male supremacy, can I do any less? Athena and I raise the white flag and say, "I surrender"! But we lie. No, no. We perform. I was wrong, you see, that women cannot act. We can, and every day. And if we are good at it, if we learn our lines well and speak them sweetly, we regain something of what we have lost. (Mask up) "I am always for the male with all my heart." (Mask down, winks broadly) Ahhhha!

Julia the Gnostic

(Reading letter)

This letter from Tertullian!

"Dear Julia. My visit to you was not without pleasure, but oh, dear cousin, I weep that you have fallen into the hands of the heretics. Here it has been only two hundred years since the death of our Lord Jesus, and already so many have fallen away . . ."

He thinks I have fallen. I feel I have flown, so like a bird!

"That you count yourself now with the Gnostics breaks my heart, dear Julia. I could hardly bear to sit in the congregation and have a woman, even my cousin whom I love, act as a priest in celebrating the eucharist — oh, Julia, do not be so immodest. You know it is not permitted for a woman to teach, undertake healings, even to baptize! And oh, the prayers you offer!"

(Puts letter down)

How I wish Jesus were here to teach us still. He was so revolutionary. He saw everyone — certainly women — with new eyes.

And what of your eyes? How do you see me? You have come here filled with curiosity. And are you also filled with superstition and prejudice? We will find out at the service this evening to which you are all invited. Will you come? And when I, a woman, pronounce the words of consecration, extend to you the sacred emblem, will you look at my woman's hand and see the hand of God, or will you recoil? I will read your faces and I will know.

The rabbis wrote, "It is well for those whose children are male, but ill for those whose children are female." But not Jesus. No. He talked with women openly, told them first of his mission, came to them first upon his rising. There was a woman who had been unclean for years, and he actually allowed her to touch him. Touch him! There was Mary, who sat at his feet to learn, just like a man, when the Torah clearly says women are not to learn And her sister Martha said, "Jesus, make her help me in the kitchen," and he said, "No, no, let her be, this is more important."

Jesus was so surprisingly generous to women that one cannot help thinking had he lived on he would have given them more and more, not less and less.

Now, that prayer that I spoke. "From Thee, Father, and through Thee, Mother, the two immortal names, Parents of the divine being . . ."

Do you know the "Gospel to the Hebrews"? Well, the orthodox churches have thrown it out. But it tells of Jesus speaking not only of his Father, but of his Mother, the Holy Spirit. And John's vision in the apocryphon. "John, John, I am the one who is with you always. I am the Father. I am the Mother. I am the Son."

I have had no vision. But I know. This is the secret of the Gnostics. To know. To know oneself at the deepest level is simultaneously to know God. I know myself, and I am female, and so I know the femaleness of God, as a man knows God's maleness. And the femaleness of God is wonderful. It is gentle, and it is powerful. Oh, I can imagine God as Mother. I see — a hand setting out in the sun a little plant that is a thousand olive trees. I see fingers weaving a cloth that is a universe of flowers, rainbows, oceans, grass, the horns and hooves of cattle. I see a wonderful shoulder rocking a baby that is the millions of us.

Is this troubling to you? Blasphemous?

Be daring! Come with me to the service this evening. Pray with me. Let the words "Father" and "Mother" rest on your lips and let their image smile in your heart. If you cannot, if you can see no femaleness in God, you will see nothing of God in the female. But if you can, you will see God in everyone! In this face. In this hand. (Indicates hands of women in audience) Or these hands.

And what shall I write my dear Tertullian? What would Jesus say to me? Oh, yes. To take the little circle my orthodox cousin has drawn that has no place for me, and to draw around it a larger circle, that I may have a place for him. "Love one another, little flock, as I have loved you." Yes.

Paula the Christian at Ephesus

You have not heard?

Oh, you should have been here this morning! When the bishop said the words, oh, I will never forget — "It has been decreed, you may worship Mary as the Mother of God" — oh, we were transported with joy! We kissed the hands of the clergy! In all the city of Ephesus there was singing and dancing! My husband danced like a child! Men need their Mother too, you know. But women, oh, we need her most especially.

I do not like to say the word, "woman." There, I said it, and it tastes bad on my tongue. Pttt-pttt! I know, as St. Clement said, and I hear it often enough, that I should be overwhelmed with shame at the very thought that I am a woman. Pttt-pttt! And I am ashamed. Oh, dear God, I am! And I know I am irredeemable, for I do not even have a soul to save — Augustine has made that quite clear!

And I know that I am once again Eve, the source of all evil, except for whom we would still be living in the Garden of Eden. I know that, as Paul said, I was created for the man, not the man for me. I know that I am weak and frivolous and the devil's gateway, and that my very presence tempts men with vile thoughts beyond enduring, and *I am sorry*!

But I make good bread! And I have produced six sons! Truthfully, I quite enjoy being a woman, until they tell me how ashamed I ought to be.

I wonder now if Mary had a soul? If we may worship her, that must mean, not only she *was*, but she *is*! What a grand thought, that *one* of us *made it*! I will have to ask the bishop!

Oh, but Mary was unusual. I could not aspire to be as she. We are under a threefold curse, women are. We are accursed if we are barren, for we exist only to give children. We are accursed if we conceive, for this is the nature of original sin. And we are accursed by the pains of childbirth. But Mary escaped all three! Imagine! She is virgin and fruitful! She conceives in holiness! She gives birth without pain! We have never known such a woman! And to think that from today she is in the heavens for us that we may worship her . . . !

God is — well, God is God and I would say nothing against him. But God can be harsh. God is stern with the men, but he seems to be especially stern with the women.

I have thought of poor Fausta, wife to the great emperor Constantine. He suspected her of committing adultery, and so he put her in a cauldron of water and had it brought to a slow boil until she died. Now, I know he was a good Christian and she ought not to have given him cause for concern, but it does seem a little — harsh.

I am safe, I think, for I am not important like Fausta, and I am not intelligent like Hypatia. Oh, Hypatia!

The church, you see, is the only source of truth,

and so it has to control all other sources, which may very well be of the devil, there is no guarantee. It has closed down the ancient Greek academies and burned the great library there, the books of poets, philosophers, and scholars, and I can understand that, for what authority has a poet or a scholar?

The great school of philosophy in Alexandria was pillaged. The head of this school was Hypatia, and that was her mistake. Well, being a woman was her first mistake, and her second mistake was to become a scholar and actually head a school. A woman is not to head, that is not her calling. But, according to talk, Hypatia was exceptionally learned and eloquent, very charming and beautiful, all of which attracted a large number of students to her lectures. Well, she was mathematician, logician, astronomer, philosopher, all this and a woman too!

Well, the bishop of Alexandria — and I am not speaking against the bishop, for he is the bishop — became very upset that Hypatia was commanding such respect, for what authority had she? And I can understand this! So, after a particularly inflammatory sermon against this woman, he urged his congregation not to allow such an unfeminine, un-Christian monster to live. They poured out of his church. They found Hypatia in her school, tore off her clothes, scraped the flesh from her bones with oyster shells, then burned what was left.

Now, I know her behavior was unwomanly. I can understand that. But . . .

Constantine ordered all the goddess temples destroyed. Oh, we have such a wonderful temple to Diana and we refused to destroy it, for we have had Diana for centuries! Large crowds gathered and we besieged the bishops. Oh, we were angry! We cried, "Give us our Diana of the Ephesians!" I felt like the woman in the book of Jeremiah, who cried out to him, "Let us worship the Queen of Heaven!" Jeremiah said, "No, no! She is an abomination!" But our church fathers are kinder to us. Well, they saw, I think, what Jeremiah did not see, that we hunger for our Mother as we do for good bread, and we will not be content with a stone!

So they told us that we could have Diana, but that her real name was Mary and we were to call her that! They re-dedicated the shrine to the virgin Mary. Well, they baptized the temple! So now we say the word "Mary," but we think "Diana" in our hearts.

And today they have told us we may call her Mother, the Mother of God, the Mother of us all. You should have seen the dancing! We may pray to her. We may reach for her consoling, maternal arms. Oh, it is hard to be a woman and not have a woman to reach to!

Mary *must* have had a soul. I will *have* to ask the bishop!

And after intermission, we will continue the quest.

ct Two

It is important to me that men feel included on this journey, because we are all in this thing together. Now, I put a microphone in the men's room to get some feedback at intermission, and I heard, "Hey, I don't do any of that stuff! Do you rape women?" "Heck no! None of this is my fault. But, boy, am I gonna get it when we get home!"

No, no. On behalf of all the women in this play, I want to thank the men in the audience who are working with us to make a better world for us all. Let's hear it for the good men! Yes!

(Takes out witch's chains)
And we have made progress.
From this dungeon —
can you smell the dank and the rot and the death?
— from this dungeon, we have made progress.

Genevieve the Witch

It is said that if you look into my eyes, an enchantment will bring you evil. You may suddenly develop leprosy. Your cow may die. You may find yourself unable to copulate with your wife or your husband. If you are not wearing your bag of salt, consecrated on Palm Sunday, I would advise you not to look into my eyes.

Old Peter foolishly forgot this precaution as he was arresting Helen on behalf of the Inquisition, and the next day she caused him to fall down a flight of stairs, which he proved by torturing her until she confirmed it. And until she confessed that yes, she was in love with the devil. And so were nineteen of her fellow townswomen, each of whom was stretched until she produced names of others, who produced names of others. It was remarkable how many women in one village had lain with Satan! Having thus righteously confessed, Helen was rescued from the chamber — and burned.

No. I will bypass the chamber, thank you. I choose to go directly to the stake. Which I will do before the sun sets.

And so you think that I have lied too? No.

A woman who is old, which I confess to being — lame, which I am most especially in the months of winter — poor, which indeed is true — a woman rumored to have found pleasure with her husband, for a woman who knows pleasure of the body is surely a witch, and God knows that was the only pleasure the miserable man gave me! — a woman spotted on the skin with witchmarks, oh, I have those — and with eyes of an unusually pale blue, which you see I have — but do not look into my eyes! — unless you are wearing your bag of salt consecrated on Palm Sunday — such a woman, it is thought, *must* be a witch. Few of them are. But I am.

"It is said you question the authority of the church," they said.

"It is true," I said. "The church may go to hell for all of me. It is a church of men, and it gives me no place and no voice."

"It is said you practice the ancient religion of pagans."

"It is true. I am high priestess to the moon Goddess."

"It is said you heal."

"Aye! I heal!"

"Do you not know the blessing witch is even worse for the land than the destroying witch?"

"Fool's words from fool's mouths," I said.

They clapped me in irons then. It will not do, you know, for a woman to speak up to a man of the church. Exodus, chapter twenty-two, verse eighteen, "Thou shalt not suffer a witch to live."

I am guilty. Maybe somewhere there is a woman who is a lover of the devil, but I have never met her. The witches that I know — we heal!

For centuries no one minded us. We were the wise women, priestesses of healing shrines, peasant healers, and they came to us, the mighty, the royal, for our knowledge and our herbs. And we kept alive some near-forgotten secret of the gracious Goddess, who gives the gift of joy to the heart, who is the beauty of the green earth and the white moon amongst the stars and the mystery of the waters, the soul of Nature.

She has whispered the secrets of healing to the mothers back and back and back. I give ergot for labor pain, though the church has banned it, saying a woman must suffer, but I give it anyway. I give belladonna to stop a miscarriage. Digitalis for the heart. And when I have nothing to give, I listen, I sense, and I do what I feel. And this is what frightens them the most — that I should listen, not to the doctrines of the church, but to the voice within.

Still they allowed us for centuries. Then — "You cannot heal," they said, "for you have not studied." But to study we would have to go to the university, and to go to the university we would have to become a man, and to make a woman into a man is something for which I have no secrets.

So when a doctor heals it is of God, and when a wise woman heals it is of the devil. When they use their magical cures, holy-water, crucifixes, it is a blessing. And when we use our charms, though our charms may work better than theirs, it is a curse. Their miracles are of saints, ours of demons. Their visions from heaven, ours from hell. I have heard — you may have heard, for the whole land knows — of a young girl, Joan of Lorraine, who was burned for her visions, though she did a great work for France.

Oh, a woman of power — she will burn!

Let me not scream as the flames move higher and higher. Nature, our Mother who sent me forth, wilt thou take me again, and let the wind be westerly after the flames have done, that I might become one with my little forest — and finally know peace!

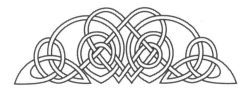

The witch showed up at rehearsal last week

wearing a button she'd found someplace —

Berkeley —must have been Berkeley

where she found this button — and it read,

"If they can send one man to the moon,

why can't they send them all?"

But the rest of us talked to her,

made her hand it over, give it up.

I know that sounds good to some of you,

but — not the answer.

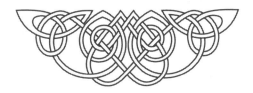

Running Cloud
the Native American

In the beginning was Thinking Woman, who has always existed. Thinking Woman sends thoughts outward into space and whatever she thinks comes into being.

She thought the rocks and the clouds and the snow and the juniper trees, and the clear rivers, and they appeared.

She thought the rabbit and the deer and the fish and the wolf and the buffalo and they walked on the earth or swam in the river.

She thought the turquoise and the shells and the silver and all that is beautiful and it happened as she thought it would.

She thought the medicine for healing.

She thought me.

She thought you.

She thought all the children and all the women and all the men, who think of her in return and in gratitude.

She thought the words that I am speaking to you now.

hoebe
the Shaker

(Sings, shaking)

> Oh, I love Mother, I love her power.
> I know 'twill help me in every trying hour.
> Help me to shake off, help me to break off
> Help me to shake off every band and fetter!

That song is my gift! You know that? It was given to me right here in the field where I was gatherin' herbs with the sisters, and I stand up and I shake and I sing, "Oh, I love Mother . . ."

You don't find no Shaker loves Mother more'n me! 'Cause it was Mother Ann Lee that shamed the white man that owned me into lettin' me go as a free woman. But Mother Ann say I don't have to go with her unless I wants to, and I say, "Oh, yeah! I wants to!" So there was a miracle that day.

And my first night there, I cry, 'cause I was thinking of my three little children that was sold away from me, and Mother Ann come in and she put her arms around me and she ast me if I was sold away from my mother and I say yes, I was, and she say then I must hold to the breast of the Heavenly Mother, who has never sold a child and never will.

And I say I never heard of such a Mother, and Mother Ann ast me if I was born of a father *and* a mother, and I say of course, and she say that I must look up through nature to God, that our natural parents are like the Perfect Parents who created us, our *Father* and *Mother* which are in Heaven! You ever heard of such a thing? Well, I was near struck dumb! And Mother Ann say, "Well, child, do you see the human world and the animal world all walkin' around lookin' like they was formed out of three masculine beings?"

And I say, "Why, no, everything comes in twos, don't it, right down to the little field mice that are male and female."

And she say, "That right, child, and God is the Eternal Two, and when the Father and Mother are both near to us, it is the season of love."

Well, I stay awake cryin', it was so beautiful.

And then I slept, and in my sleep I remember — oh, I remember what my Mama sang to me and her Mama sang to her, and all the Mamas sang back to Africa — about that great, shinin' black Mother of us all! And in my sleep I lay in the lap of that Great Mother and she stroke my hair, and she say, "Shhhh, honey, it gonna be all right . . . someday it all gonna be all right. 'Cause you is my baby and I is your Mama forever!" And she sing me a lullaby, and oh, I slept so good.

I a Deaconess, you know that? We don't have no Deacons without no Deaconesses. And we don't have no Elders without no Elderesses. I was the lowest of the low. I was a woman and I was black, but God has raised me high. And Mother Ann is our Elect Lady, the mother to us all, and we sit at her feet on a carpet of her love, soft as velvet, and we learn from her.

Why, she been beaten and flogged and stoned and imprisoned and dragged by her heels, and she forgive them all and she say, "Love your enemies!" I have seen her rise in power and calm a angry mob. I have seen her speak to the Indians in their own tongue, like a miracle. And I have stood with her as we lay on hands and healed a woman with legs swollen like that!

Oh, bless the day Mother found me on the auction block and bought me for God. I sing and I dance and I shake off the past. And I rejoice in the gifts!

(Sings)

Help me to shake off, help me to break off,
Help me to shake off every band and fetter!

You have to understand how excited I was
to meet Emma Smith.

Where I go to church,
about once a year we sing a wonderful hymn,
written by somebody very close to Emma,
and some of the words are:

"In the heavens, are parents single?
No, the thought makes reason stare.
Truth is reason, truth eternal
Tells me I've a Mother there.
When I leave this frail existence,
When I lay this mortal by,
Father, Mother, may I meet you
In your royal courts on high."

Emma Smith the Mormon First Lady

You will not find another shawl like this in all the city of Nauvoo. Joseph gave it to me. It is beautiful, isn't it? I wore it last month when I went to St. Louis, but mostly I just take it out to look at.

Oh, they stare at me in St. Louis, I can tell you, and not for my shawl. "Look," they whisper, "there goes Mrs. Smith, the wife of Joe, the Mormon Prophet. Why do you suppose she stays with him?"

How many women are his wives now? Oh, you would like to know, wouldn't you? Eleven that I know of, and more you can be certain.

But Joseph loves *me*! And no other woman in Nauvoo has a shawl like this.

Don't bother turning away your eyes. "Poor, degraded, mindless Mormon woman," you are saying.

No! You don't understand. The gospel that Joseph restored is for the women as well as the men, and already we have made such strides that some of the brethren complain. Joseph ordained and set apart many women to lay on hands, anoint with oil, heal the sick. He tells us that we, like Miriam and Deborah, may have the gift of prophecy, receive revelation for ourselves, become queens and priestesses. No one can say that the poor, Mormon women are downtrodden.

Well, it is true that after we had ground up our china to make the plaster for the Kirtland temple shine, after we had woven the veils, we were not invited in — until some time after the brethren. We are *always* after the brethren. And, yes, I have sometimes had my fill of Brigham pointing out that women were made to be led and directed and to submit cheerfully, for we have not the degree of light and intelligence that our husbands have. But, I say all in good time, and for now let us count our blessings.

Joseph has even taught — we don't speak much of this, for it would be another stone for our enemies to cast against us, and I ask you to be careful where you tell it — Joseph has even taught that in the heavens there is not only a Heavenly Father, there's a Heavenly Mother, as well. "How could there be a Father?" he asks, "If there were not also a Mother, as divine as he?"

And he tells us that we might someday become — like them! Imagine! In some eternity — I might become a Goddess!

You are judging him harshly. Yes, you are. "How can a man who so exalts women," you are saying, "subject his own wife, whom he claims to love, and the wives of his followers, who are good and tender-hearted women, to the monstrous evil of polygamy? How can he claim this comes of God?"

That is what you are saying, isn't it? But no, you are wrong. I have said that too, but I was wrong. I was listening to Satan, who seeks to destroy me!

If you knew Joseph you would know why I love him as much as any woman has ever loved a

man. I disobeyed my father and eloped with him.
No better man, save Jesus, ever walked this earth.
Joseph is forever giving away his boots, coming
home again barefoot. He is a very — loving man.
No, that is not it! God commanded it that
righteous seed. . . .

I was a stumbling block to the whole Church!
Joseph told me — God told me in a revelation to
Joseph, "Let mine handmaid, Emma Smith, receive
all those that have been given unto my servant
Joseph. And if she will not abide this
commandment, she shall be destroyed, saith the
Lord, your God."

Oh, I fought! But I did not want to be
destroyed! So I agreed. I chose the two Partridge
sisters, Emily and Eliza, whom I had taken in
before as my daughters. I instructed them in the
beautiful principle of patriarchal marriage. I stood
and watched as Judge Adams, a high priest in the
Church, married them to my husband.

But no other woman in Nauvoo has a shawl. . . !

How did Sarah do it? She gave Hagar to
Abraham. Did she love him? How does the
Muslim woman do it today? Millions of them.

Oh, I think sometimes of the wife of God the
Father, that Mother Joseph has told us of. Well, if
what Joseph teaches is true, that as we are now,
God once was and as God is now we may become,
then — then God our Father must have numerous
wives, more even than Joseph!

I would like to speak to the Father's first wife!
She must not have been so rebellious as I. And I
would say to her, "How did you do it?"

Mrs. Stanton asked me

to make her introduction very short,

as she has spent the whole evening backstage,

pacing, listening and getting more and more upset.

Well, you will see.

But I must tell you just a few things

about this very remarkable woman . . . .

(is interrupted).

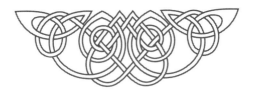

Elizabeth Cady Stanton the American Feminist

Enough, enough, Madam, enough! Now, are there any questions — from the audience, please?

Yes, the gentleman at the back of the hall.

Hmmm. "Mrs. Stanton," he says, "tell us about the new Bible you and the devil have written."

I must disappoint the good gentleman. What I have written is only a commentary on the Bible. And it was written, sir, by Ellen, Louisa, Ursula, Frances and myself. His Satanic Majesty was not invited to the committee!

The Bible, ladies and gentlemen, has been made authority for the grossest wrongs, from war and slavery to polygamy and the subjection of women, even the beating of a wife every fortnight with a horsewhip. Well, I wrote an article last winter on that new amusement, the bicycle, and many timid souls were greatly distressed. Should women ride? What are God's intentions concerning *woman and the bicycle*?

What? Yes, he says it is clearly out of her sphere, would be immodest and whatever would she wear!

Isn't it wonderful, women, that we have men to

define for us our sphere? It appears to me that a man
has enough in this life to find his own calling without
being taxed to decide where every *woman* belongs!

Now. You may think me hostile to the Bible.
No. Only inasmuch as the Bible is hostile to me.
The principles there that teach love, charity, justice,
equality for the whole human family, the wonderful
words of Jesus, the Golden Rule, I embrace with
my whole heart. But I will not blame God for the
codes and creeds that degrade women. And we
could argue 'til the cows come home as to who is
more to blame, the Christians or the Jews, and I
say they're *both* to blame!

And yet — there is a seed, planted in the first
chapter of Genesis, that would elevate woman. "So
God created man in his own image, in the image of
God created he him; male and female created he
them." A simultaneous creation of both sexes, in
the image of God! A plain declaration of the
existence of the feminine element in the Godhead,
equal in power and glory with the masculine. The
Heavenly Father — and *Mother*!

Would one of you please locate your smelling
salts should they be needed by the man at the back
of the hall? What? — woman in the Godhead when
she ought not even to ride a bicycle? Hmmmph!

I say that the first step in the elevation of
woman is the recognition of an ideal Heavenly
Mother, to whom their prayers should be addressed,
as well as to a Father — the first step!

But the clergy have long since forgotten that
both were made in the image of a God who must *be*
both! With a few notable exceptions.

Well, the Reverend Theodore Parker — such

a good man, Theodore Parker — spoke of, "The dear Heavenly Mother, who never slumbers, but who cares continually for the great housekeeping of all the world." Now, don't you like that! "The great housekeeping of all the world!"

But most of the clergy have forgotten her, and women are the chief support of the very institution that makes their emancipation impossible. The woman and the slave are of similar fate, you know, except that the woman looks longingly toward heaven, while the more philosophical slave long ago set out for Canada!

Yes? The woman with the baby, please.

She asks if I have been unable to find a husband and therefore I complain. No, Madam, thank you, I have a husband and on the whole he is wonderfully good to me, as are my seven children. It is not I who lacks a husband. It is the world, the church that lacks a Mother, and without her their behavior is disgraceful! She ought to stand them all in the corner!

In 1840 I attended an anti-slavery convention in London. The British abolitionists there refused to allow the female delegates to sit on the main floor or to vote. William Lloyd Garrison, another good man, joined us in the balcony in protest, but my own husband, I am sorry to say, acquiesced in this shameful arrangement. This humiliation convinced me and a sister delegate, Lucretia Mott, that there were others besides the Negroes who needed attention, and thus we conceived the idea of the first woman's rights convention, held eight years later in Seneca Falls, New York, in 1848.

Yes, yes. The lady taps her wedding ring and

says, "I have all the rights I need." Oh, my friend
Susan Anthony and I discuss this often. Sometimes
the severest enemy to woman is not man, but
woman herself!

When Elizabeth Blackwell, the first female
doctor in this country, attended medical school, the
women at the boarding houses refused to speak to
her! When the *women* passed her on the sidewalk,
they picked up their skirts so as not to touch her!
For shame! Women kiss the chains that bind
them! And they tell me that to ask for more than
the men deign to give them does not seem—polite.

Polite! Men and angels give me patience! If I
could not speak and declare my mind, I would die
of a woman's rights convulsion!

Yes, I am a radical. I have been ridiculed and
criticized for forty years. Iron has entered my soul.
I say require of the state that we be given full
citizenship and that it happen now. And I say
require of the church the same thing, to acknowledge
that man and woman were created in the image of
God and given dominion over this earth, but none
over each other. None over each other!

Some of the women objected as we titled our
newspaper, "The Revolution." We could, perhaps,
have titled it, "The Rosebud." But we titled it "The
Revolution," because it smells like a revolution.
And a revolution it is, marching forward in the
majesty of truth to confront the stronghold of the
kingdom of darkness.

The gentleman at the back of the hall
expressed the opinion that woman always has been
and always will be in subjection. My dear,
conservative friend, wipe the dew from your

spectacles! She enjoyed unlimited freedom for many centuries, until man gained the upper hand. But new forces are gathering, and soon—man and woman will reign as equals on earth, as the Heavenly Father and Heavenly Mother reign as equals in the heavens!

Well, they are turning off the lights and we had the hall only until nine o'clock. If someone would be so kind as to help me with the stairs? Susan has a gospel of work and diet and exercise, and I am an infidel on all but the work part, as you can see. I thank you.

Don't you wish she went to *your* church?
Or maybe was running for president?

I did worry some about bringing
these next two women here together.
There's such a lot of pain there.
But they're sisters in spite of themselves.
In spite of themselves,
these two women are sisters.

ilda the Nazi Woman

Ah! You overheard as I was sending Wilhelm and Hannah to bed. Yes, it took some getting used to, but now I see the wisdom.

"Fuhrer, my Fuhrer, I thank thee today for my daily bread. Thy Third Reich comes, thy will alone is law upon earth. We will obey thee even with our lives and praise thee. Heil, Hitler!"

Do you see? My motherhood medal. It is gold. With my fifth child, I was given a medal. Bronze. With my sixth, silver. With my seventh, gold. One of Hitler's goals is to rid society of the Jew and the New Woman. I am not the New Woman. *She* has given up her femininity. *She* demands a place in public decision making. *She* seeks paid labor outside the home. *She* believes that suffrage for women was a step forward. But Hitler sees through all this! He has emancipated us from our emancipation and allows us to be home, where we belong.

Femininity would destroy the revolution! I heard with my own ears our Fuhrer say, "The Nazi revolution will be an entirely male event!" That is good. We are now, you know, the Fatherland, not the Motherland, for the state must be strong as a man is strong, hardened against a temptation to femininity. The man in the state. The woman in the home. There is room for softness in the home.

I do feel sorry for those who are not racially fit to become mothers or fathers, for those who must be sterilized or relieved of a burdensome life — the cripple, the feminized man, perhaps even the Jewish woman that I have known since we were girls, Rebecca and her husband Chaim and their children. I do feel sorry if that is to be, and sometimes I wonder if . . . but that is the woman in me, and I must shout the woman down! No! No! This is the business of the state and well left to those who are strong enough to do it.

I had the women from the the National Association of Homemakers over this evening. We read from "Mein Kampf." We sewed brown shirts for the S.R. It is good to have a sisterhood whose goal is unquestioning obedience to the movement.

My husband will be home for the weekend, any minute now. He is at Auschwitz on special assignment of the Fuhrer! He does not tell me. I do not ask, for it is not my concern. But it must be hard, for when he was last here there was a faraway look in his eyes and his hand shook. My heart went out to him.

I cleaned the rooms today, though they were already spotless. When my husband comes, I like to make things nice for him. He serves the Fuhrer and I serve him! It is good. Yah?

Rebecca the Jewish Woman

(Polishing candelabra)

Chaim?

I worry more than Chaim does. He says, "If the Nazis kill my body, they cannot touch my soul." He worries only that he does not have a son to say prayers for him when he is dead. Breaks my heart to hear Chaim pray so for a son. I pray for a son too, even though we are told God does not listen to women — I pray for a son.

When I was little I always wished that I was a boy — that I could make aliot, be called to the Torah service, be counted in the minyan to make up a quorum for prayer. But do not think that I am barred from heaven for being a woman. Oh, no. If Chaim is sufficiently godly, he brings me in with him. And so his godliness is what I devote my life to. He serves God, and I serve him. It is good.

He would not be late tonight of all nights. We are *always* together on Shabbat! The Kabbalah says . . . well, most Jews have forgotten the Kabbalah, but Chaim and I find it rather lovely. Friday night, the Kabbalah says, a queenly visitor enters even the most humble abode. She is the Holy Shekhinah, Shabbat Queen, the feminine part of God.

Well, I must light these candles without him.
(Covers head, lights candles)
"Barukh Atah Adonai Eloheinu . . . B'tzivanu
. . . Ner Shel Shabbat."
Chaim says the Holy Shekhinah is only
poetry. The Shekhinah has been banished, you
know. She is in exile, and God mourns the loss as
only God can mourn. But I mourn too. Who
banished her? Do you know? And why? The
Kabbalah says that when a man sins he causes a
separation between the male and female in the
deity, which, in turn, leads to a universal disaster.

Is that it? Have we sinned? The Shekhinah
has been exiled from God and the boots of evil
march up and down the streets of Berlin! And I
listen for the step of Chaim, and I pray that my
little children will not face the horrors I have heard.
I pray, even though I am a woman!

But, on Shabbat — we rejoice! And we light
our candles. And we bake our sacred, braided
bread. And after midnight — the Kabbalah says —
that after midnight a man and his wife must be
coupled in the marriage bed, because their coupling
on Shabbat assists God and his Shekhinah to
couple and to be one as they should be one. And
from their oneness comes the souls of humans.
And from their oneness the world will be healed!

So that is why Chaim would never, never stay
away from home on Shabbat! In a moment — he will,
I know he will—he will come in through the dusk and
smile and open his arms and say to me and to Shabbat,
Come in peace, O crown of her husband
In joy and in jubilation.
Come, O Bride . . . Come, O Bride!

We do not blow out Sabbath candles.

arie
the Therapist

You know, I have a friend that every time I tell her a story like this one, she says, "Ha! You see? The return of the Goddess!" Well, sometimes I do think that after all the pain — I get a front row seat to a miracle.

Now, Daniel — he began coming to me for therapy because he was afraid his wife was going to leave him. And he was right. She told me, "My husband never talks to me, never listens, never shares anything real. He works, he watches television, he runs — but he doesn't relate."

The first day that Daniel came to this office, he said almost nothing. He had no language to express his inner life. You'd have thought he had no inner life, but he had. And there was pain in that life.

Daniel was, you might say, the wounded child of wounded parents. The sins of the fathers, you know. Oh, and the mothers. He had very clear ideas of what a man was to be and what a woman was to be. He had no memory of his father ever doing anything really tender, and no memory of his mother ever doing anything really powerful. I asked him if he didn't miss that. He shrugged his shoulders, but then he began to remember.

He remembered at age eight lying in bed after a burst appendix, very sick, near to dying, his mother holding him, his father standing in the doorway saying, "Hey, hey, you'll be okay." He wanted so much for his father to come in and hold him too. And he remembered at age eleven being forced to go deer hunting for the first time. He didn't want to go. He remembered kneeling there by that bleeding deer, crying, his father coming over, swearing at him, pushing him down, calling him a girl.

And he remembered that he hadn't even gone to a professional barber until he was well past his teens, because his father cut hair in the kitchen and that meant that once a month he could sit there and have his father touch him, and he liked that.

And through all this, he remembered his mother — so powerless to do anything to protect him or to make any demands for herself. Do you know his most vivid memory of his mother? Her standing at the kitchen sink, peeling potatoes and crying. Most vivid memory.

Well, to change himself —. You know somebody once told me it takes just one therapist to change a light globe. But the light globe has to really want to change. No. For people — for Daniel to change, he had to change his parents, his models, and they've been dead for years. So we've been working on that right here in this room. Daniel has been going inside of himself to that place that knows what his parents would have done for him if only they could have.

This evening he closed his eyes and held some conversations. He said, "Dad, if you could go back and do it over again, if you could be a better father to me, what would you do?" And he watched while his father took him back into that forest, knelt down with him by that bleeding deer, put an arm around him, and he said, "I'm sorry. We don't have to do this." And his father came in from the doorway — didn't even know how, but he managed to put his arms around his son, and he said, "Don't die, Danny. I love you. I love you."

And Daniel asked the same question of his mother. He said, "Mother, what would you do if you could go back and be a better mother to me?"

Well, she put down the potato peeler and dried her eyes and marched out and stood by that truck and she said, "No, you're not taking Daniel hunting. He doesn't want to go and he doesn't have to go. And what's more, when you get back from hunting, we're going to go on that family vacation you've been promising us for ten years. We're going to go up to the Tetons, and we're going to have a wonderful time, and you don't have to come if you don't want to, but I hope you will!"

Then she went in and sat down at the piano. Daniel knew she used to play, but not since he was very small and only just a little, but she played — Mozart and Beethoven — and it was glorious! And Daniel cried — the little boy, yes — but the big man too, right here in this room — cried, so happy finally to be held in the arms of both his mother and his father — a father who was not afraid of those things we have made the big mistake of labeling feminine things — and a mother who was not afraid of being a woman of power.

And as I walked Daniel to the door just a few minutes ago, I looked up and there was the moon, so full. The return of the Goddess? Maybe my friend was right.

arol Lynn Pearson

On another day, I spoke to my children about God again. This time not alone — surrounded by my sisters, filled with their hunger, their anguish, their triumph and their determination. Again I began with my eldest.

"Emily," I said, "close your eyes. I want you to call up that picture of God. Is he still there with a stern face and doesn't like you much?"

"Hmmm. Doesn't like me too much."

"Oh, Emily, that's not God! That's somebody else's idea of God. Paint it over, Em. Paint a new God!"

"Oh! Okay. Then — I guess I'll make him be — a ballet dancer. And he's not too old, sort of young. And he has a beautiful, kind face."

"Does he like you?"

"Oh, he loves me. And he would like to dance with me!"

"Now, keep your eyes closed, Em. How would you feel about adding to your God-man a God-woman? Let her be as perfect and as beautiful as he is. Could you see them? Could you see them together?"

"Oh — yes, I could. Oh!"

I watched her face as Emily staged a wonderful ballet — with herself and God and Goddess whirling together through the galaxies.

My sisters watched too. These and the one hundred million who ought to be with us today. I felt them press in so close. For my daughter is not only mine — she is theirs. She's their hope and their healing. We all watched, as behind Emily's eyelids the divine family was reunited — and the dear Heavenly Mother held out to us all her great arms.

Dear Goddess. Oh, Mother — we have missed you. Weave with us a new morning.

Welcome home!

arol Lynn Pearson was first a performer, then a writer, and now, with *Mother Wove the Morning*, combines those two gifts in what she feels is the most important work of her professional life.

She is the author of five books of poetry, which to date have sold over 250,000 copies, most recently *Women I Have Known and Been.*

An autobiography, *Goodbye, I Love You*, tells the story of her life with her husband Gerald, the struggle his homosexuality brought to their marriage, their divorce and his subsequent death from AIDS in Carol Lynn's home, where she was caring for him.

She has been a popular guest on such shows as "The Oprah Winfrey Show," "Good Morning, America," "Charles Kurault," "Sally Jesse Raphael" and "Geraldo." She has been featured in "People" magazine and "Woman's Day," and is in demand across the country as a speaker.

Other works include educational motion pictures, such as "Cipher in the Snow," winner of twenty-nine national and international awards, and children's plays, two that were commissioned by Robert Redford's Sundance Theatre.

Ms. Pearson received her B.A. and M.A. in drama at Brigham Young University, where she twice received the "Best Actress" award. She subsequently toured the Orient performing for the State Department and also performed at the prestigious Utah Shakespeare Festival.

Since its birth in 1989, *Mother Wove the Morning* has played in extended runs in numerous states and in Dublin, Ireland. The play was selected by Margarita Papandreou, former first lady of Greece, to be a featured presentation at the "First International Minoan Celebration of Partnership" on Crete in October of 1992. *Mother Wove the Morning* is now available on video. Ms. Pearson has worked and lived in Walnut Creek, California with her four children since 1976.

Also by Carol Lynn Pearson

Goodbye, I Love You, Random House, autobiography

One On The Seesaw: The Ups and Downs of a Single Parent Family, Random House, autobiography

Beginnings, Bookcraft, poetry

The Growing Season, Bookcraft, poetry

A Widening View, Bookcraft, poetry

I Can't Stop Smiling, Bookcraft, poetry

Women I Have Known and Been, Aspen Press, poetry

A Lasting Peace, Deseret Book, juvenile novel

A Stranger for Christmas, Bookcraft, novelette

Daughters of Light, Bookcraft, history

The Flight and the Nest, Bookcraft, history

Will I Ever Forget This Day?, Bookcraft, diary excerpts

My Turn on Earth, Embryo Music, family musical

Pegora the Witch, Anchorage Press, children's play

Don't Count Your Chickens Until They Cry Wolf, Anchorage Press, children's play

I Believe in Make Believe, Anchorage Press

ajor Sources

Paleolithic:
The Great Cosmic Mother, Monica Sjoo & Barbara Mor;
The Chalice and the Blade, Riane Eisler.

Rachel:
Sarah the Priestess, the First Matriarch of Genesis,
Savina J. Teubal; Genesis, chapter 31.

Midianite Virgin:
Numbers, chapter 31.

Egyptian Priestess:
The Feminine Dimension of the Divine,
Joan Chamberlain Engelsman.

Levite's Concubine:
Judges, chapter 19.

Greek:
The Chalice and the Blade, Eisler;
"The Eumenides," Aeschylus;
Lost Goddesses of Early Greece, Charlene Spretnak.

Gnostic:
The Gnostic Gospels, Elaine Pagels.

Christian at Ephesus:
Woman's Encyclopedia of Myths and Secrets,
Barbara Walker.

Witch:
When God Was a Woman, Merlin Stone;
Woman's Encyclopedia, Walker.

Native American:
Ceremony, Leslie Marmon Silko.

Shaker:
Ann the Word, Nard Reeder Campion;
The Gift to be Simple, Songs, Dances and Rituals of the American Shakers, Edward Deming Andrews.

Mormon:
Emma Smith: Mormon Enigma,
Linda Newell and Valeen Avery;
A History of Joseph Smith by His Mother,
Lucy Mack Smith.

Feminist:
Eighty Years and More, Elizabeth Cady Stanton;
The Woman's Bible, Stanton.

Nazi:
Mothers in the Fatherland, Claudia Koonz.

Jewish:
The Hebrew Goddess, Raphael Patai.

Therapist:
The Natural Superiority of Women, Ashley Montague;
We, Robert A. Johnson.